Francis Frith's
Black Country

Photographic Memories

Francis Frith's
Black Country

Dorothy Nicolle
and Alan Rose

FRITH
BOOK Co

First published in the United Kingdom in 2002 by
Frith Book Company Ltd

ISBN 1-85937-497-2

British Library Cataloguing in Publication Data

Francis Frith's Black Country
Dorothy Nicolle and Alan Rose

Frith Book Company Ltd
Frith's Barn, Teffont,
Salisbury, Wiltshire SP3 5QP
Tel: +44 (0) 1722 716 376
Email: info@francisfrith.co.uk
www.francisfrith.co.uk

Printed and bound in Great Britain

Front Cover: Wolverhampton, Queen Street c1900 W285001

Contents

Francis Frith: Victorian Pioneer   7

Frith's Archive - A Unique Legacy   10

The Black Country - An Introduction   12

Wolverhampton   16

Around Wolverhampton   38

Walsall to West Bromwich   51

Dudley to Stourbridge   60

Index   83

Free Mounted Print Voucher   87

Francis Frith: *Victorian Pioneer*

FRANCIS FRITH, Victorian founder of the world-famous photographic archive, was a complex and multi-talented man. A devout Quaker and a highly successful Victorian businessman, he was both philosophic by nature and pioneering in outlook.

By 1855 Francis Frith had already established a wholesale grocery business in Liverpool, and sold it for the astonishing sum of £200,000, which is the equivalent today of over £15,000,000. Now a multi-millionaire, he was able to indulge his passion for travel. As a child he had pored over travel books written by early explorers, and his fancy and imagination had been stirred by family holidays to the sublime mountain regions of Wales and Scotland. 'What a land of spirit-stirring and enriching scenes and places!' he had written. He was to return to these scenes of grandeur in later years to 'recapture the thousands of vivid and tender memories', but with a different purpose. Now in his thirties, and captivated by the new science of photography, Frith set out on a series of pioneering journeys to the Nile regions that occupied him from 1856 until 1860.

Intrigue and Adventure

He took with him on his travels a specially-designed wicker carriage that acted as both dark-room and sleeping chamber. These far-flung journeys were packed with intrigue and adventure. In his life story, written when he was sixty-three, Frith tells of being held captive by bandits, and of fighting 'an awful midnight battle to the very point of surrender with a deadly pack of hungry, wild dogs'. Sporting flowing Arab costume, Frith arrived at Akaba by camel seventy years before Lawrence, where he encountered 'desert princes and rival sheikhs, blazing with jewel-hilted swords'.

During these extraordinary adventures he was assiduously exploring the desert regions bordering the Nile and patiently recording the antiquities and peoples with his camera. He was the first photographer to venture beyond the sixth cataract. Africa was still the mysterious 'Dark Continent', and Stanley and Livingstone's historic meeting was a decade into the future. The conditions for picture taking confound belief. He laboured for hours in his wicker dark-room in the sweltering heat of the desert, while the volatile chemicals fizzed dangerously in their trays. Often he was forced to work in remote tombs and caves where conditions were cooler. Back in London he exhibited his photographs and was 'rapturously cheered' by members of the Royal Society. His reputation as a photographer was made overnight. An eminent modern historian has likened their impact on the population of the time to that on our own generation of the first photographs taken on the surface of the moon.

Venture of a Life-Time

Characteristically, Frith quickly spotted the opportunity to create a new business as a specialist publisher of photographs. He lived in an era of immense and sometimes violent change. For the poor in the early part of Victoria's reign work was a drudge and the hours long, and people had precious little free time to enjoy themselves. Most had no transport other than a cart or gig at their disposal, and had not travelled far beyond the boundaries of their own town or village. However,

by the 1870s, the railways had threaded their way across the country, and Bank Holidays and half-day Saturdays had been made obligatory by Act of Parliament. All of a sudden the ordinary working man and his family were able to enjoy days out and see a little more of the world.

With characteristic business acumen, Francis Frith foresaw that these new tourists would enjoy having souvenirs to commemorate their days out. In 1860 he married Mary Ann Rosling and set out with the intention of photographing every city, town and village in Britain. For the next thirty years he travelled the country by train and by pony and trap, producing fine photographs of seaside resorts and beauty spots that were keenly bought by millions of Victorians. These prints were painstakingly pasted into family albums and pored over during the dark nights of winter, rekindling precious memories of summer excursions.

The Rise of Frith & Co

Frith's studio was soon supplying retail shops all over the country. To meet the demand he gathered about him a small team of photographers, and published the work of independent artist-photographers of the calibre of Roger Fenton and Francis Bedford. In order to gain some understanding of the scale of Frith's business one only has to look at the catalogue issued by Frith & Co in 1886: it runs to some 670 pages, listing not only many thousands of views of the British Isles but also many photographs of most European countries, and China, Japan, the USA and Canada – note the sample page shown above from the hand-written *Frith & Co* ledgers detailing pictures taken. By 1890 Frith had created the greatest specialist photographic publishing company in the world,

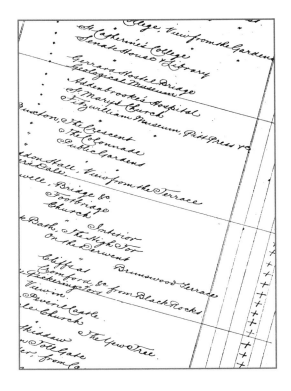

Frith's death, a new card measuring 5.5 x 3.5 inches became the standard format, but it was not until 1902 that the divided back came into being, with address and message on one face and a full-size illustration on the other. *Frith & Co* were in the vanguard of postcard development, and Frith's sons Eustace and Cyril continued their father's monumental task, expanding the number of views offered to the public and recording more and more places in Britain, as the coasts and countryside were opened up to mass travel.

Francis Frith died in 1898 at his villa in Cannes, his great project still growing. The archive he created continued in business for another seventy years. By 1970 it contained over a third of a million pictures of 7,000 cities, towns and villages. The massive photographic record Frith has left to us stands as a living monument to a special and very remarkable man.

with over 2,000 outlets – more than the combined number that Boots and W H Smith have today! The picture on the right shows the *Frith & Co* display board at Ingleton in the Yorkshire Dales. Beautifully constructed with mahogany frame and gilt inserts, it could display up to a dozen local scenes.

Postcard Bonanza

The ever-popular holiday postcard we know today took many years to develop. In 1870 the Post Office issued the first plain cards, with a pre-printed stamp on one face. In 1894 they allowed other publishers' cards to be sent through the mail with an attached adhesive halfpenny stamp. Demand grew rapidly, and in 1895 a new size of postcard was permitted called the court card, but there was little room for illustration. In 1899, a year after

Frith's Archive: *A Unique Legacy*

FRANCIS FRITH'S legacy to us today is of immense significance and value, for the magnificent archive of evocative photographs he created provides a unique record of change in 7,000 cities, towns and villages throughout Britain over a century and more. Frith and his fellow studio photographers revisited locations many times down the years to update their views, compiling for us an enthralling and colourful pageant of British life and character.

We tend to think of Frith's sepia views of Britain as nostalgic, for most of us use them to conjure up memories of places in our own lives with which we have family associations. It often makes us forget that to Francis Frith they were records of daily life as it was actually being lived in the cities, towns and villages of his day. The Victorian age was one of great and often bewildering change for ordinary people, and though the pictures evoke an impression of slower times, life was as busy and hectic as it is today.

We are fortunate that Frith was a photographer of the people, dedicated to recording the minutiae of everyday life. For it is this sheer wealth of visual data, the painstaking chronicle of changes in dress, transport, street layouts, buildings, housing, engineering and landscape that captivates us so much today. His remarkable images offer us a powerful link with the past and with the lives of our ancestors.

Today's Technology

Computers have now made it possible for Frith's many thousands of images to be accessed almost instantly. In the Frith archive today, each photograph is carefully 'digitised' then stored on a CD Rom. Frith archivists can locate a single photograph amongst thousands within seconds. Views can be catalogued and sorted under a variety of categories of place and content to the immediate benefit of researchers.

Inexpensive reference prints can be created for them at the touch of a mouse button, and a wide range of books and other printed materials assembled and published for a wider, more general readership - in the next twelve months over a hundred Frith local history titles will be published! The day-to-day workings of the archive are very different from how they were in Francis Frith's time: imagine the herculean task of sorting through eleven tons of glass negatives as Frith had to do to locate a particular sequence of pictures! Yet

See Frith at www.francisfrith.co.uk

the archive still prides itself on maintaining the same high standards of excellence laid down by Francis Frith, including the painstaking cataloguing and indexing of every view.

It is curious to reflect on how the internet now allows researchers in America and elsewhere greater instant access to the archive than Frith himself ever enjoyed. Many thousands of individual views can be called up on screen within seconds on one of the Frith internet sites, enabling people living continents away to revisit the streets of their ancestral home town, or view places in Britain where they have enjoyed holidays. Many overseas researchers welcome the chance to view special theme selections, such as transport, sports, costume and ancient monuments.

We are certain that Francis Frith would have heartily approved of these modern developments in imaging techniques, for he himself was always working at the very limits of Victorian photographic technology.

The Value of the Archive Today

Because of the benefits brought by the computer, Frith's images are increasingly studied by social historians, by researchers into genealogy and ancestory, by architects, town planners, and by teachers and schoolchildren involved in local history projects.

In addition, the archive offers every one of us an opportunity to examine the places where we and our families have lived and worked down the years. Highly successful in Frith's own era, the archive is now, a century and more on, entering a new phase of popularity.

The Past in Tune with the Future

Historians consider the Francis Frith Collection to be of prime national importance. It is the only archive of its kind remaining in private ownership and has been valued at a million pounds. However, this figure is now rapidly increasing as digital technology enables more and more people around the world to enjoy its benefits.

Francis Frith's archive is now housed in an historic timber barn in the beautiful village of Teffont in Wiltshire. Its founder would not recognize the archive office as it is today. In place of the many thousands of dusty boxes containing glass plate negatives and an all-pervading odour of photographic chemicals, there are now ranks of computer screens. He would be amazed to watch his images travelling round the world at unimaginable speeds through network and internet lines.

The archive's future is both bright and exciting. Francis Frith, with his unshakeable belief in making photographs available to the greatest number of people, would undoubtedly approve of what is being done today with his lifetime's work. His photographs, depicting our shared past, are now bringing pleasure and enlightenment to millions around the world a century and more after his death.

The Black Country - *An Introduction*

'When Satan in the Black Country
Far around him gazed,
He said, 'I never shall again
At Hell's flames be amazed.'

ORIGINALLY this little rhyme referred just to Brierley Hill, one of many towns that constitute what we now call the Black Country. However, I have reworded it slightly because it brings home to us the Black Country of 200 years ago. It is difficult for us now, some years after the introduction of Clean Air Acts, to imagine what it must have been like then, with hundreds of furnaces covering a relatively small area constantly spewing out their smoke and grime. The people who lived here must often have felt that the churchmen of the day were describing their own environment when they mentioned Hell.

But where is this Black Country? Today, people who live in Wolverhampton, for example, will often insist that their home town was never considered part of the Black Country. And yet visitors will find as they arrive that the signs for Wolverhampton proudly proclaim a welcome to the Black Country. Generally the Black Country stretches from Wolverhampton in the north, eastwards to Walsall and then south through West Bromwich and Dudley

as far as Stourbridge. This meant that the area was never defined by any political border, as it stretched between Staffordshire and Worcestershire. In the 1970s the county boundaries were re-drawn; today the Black Country lies, with neighbouring Birmingham, in the new 'county' of the West Midlands.

And what is the Black Country? The name derives from the dirt and smoke of what has for many centuries been an area of heavy industrialisation. This is not a totally new phenomenon. It was always agriculturally rather poor but rich in iron ore, coal, limestone and fireclay, and so there has been industry here for some time.

It has been estimated that in the 1600s there were already around 20,000 smiths working within a 10-mile radius of Dudley. And they all used wood. In fact, nearly 20,000 trees were needed each year just to provide the charcoal for smelting iron ore in the region. We must remember that wood was a very valuable commodity at the time, and burning it was a terrible waste – it was needed for building houses, furniture, and carts, not to mention the ships required to keep the country secure and to trade around the world.

Thus when Abraham Darby, who was born near Dudley, invented a process for smelting iron using coke rather than charcoal, he saved the nation's resources of wood. Darby made his discovery in 1709 when working in Coalbrookdale, a few miles away in Shropshire. Overnight, the Industrial Revolution began. The new ideas and techniques rapidly spread, and in next to no time this whole area boomed.

But the name of this area is still relatively new. In fact, for a long time it was known as the Iron Country. The first reference that has been found to the 'Black Country' was in a book that appeared as recently as 1860. It was such a perfect term that it was used eight years later by Elihu Burritt, then the American Consul in Birmingham, when he published a book titled 'The Black Country and its Green Borderland' – and since then the local people have tried to live it down.

Certainly there is a lot to live down. Descriptions of the region in the 17th and 18th centuries often describe scenes of a Hell on Earth. Elihu Burritt opened his book by describing it as being 'black by day and red by night'. Earlier, Thomas Carlyle had described 'a frightful scene (with) a dense cloud of pestilential smoke (where) the whole region burns like a volcano spitting fire from a thousand tubes of brick'.

But it was not just Abraham Darby's discovery that changed the world forever. Unless you can get your goods to a market, it is pointless to produce them. The 18th century was to see vast improvements in transportation systems throughout the country, and without these the Industrial Revolution could never have happened. The improvements were largely twofold – the introduction of quality roads (the early toll roads) and, far more important, the development of the canals.

The first canals were not built primarily for the transportation of finished products, however. At first they were intended for the transportation of coal – for example, when the canal between Wednesbury and Birmingham first opened in 1769 the price of coal suddenly dropped from 13 shillings to 7 shillings a ton. The canal system that linked Birmingham and the Black Country with the rest of Britain, and via our ports with the rest of the world, was what made this region so successful.

Another new age began when the first railway opened in the area in 1829. Again, it was the transportation of coal that caused it to be built – the railway linked coal mines at Pensnett Chase with the Staffordshire and Worcestershire Canal – but new lines were soon being built to transport all manner of goods (and people) around the region.

Although brought together and described more

often than not as one region, the Black Country consists of many separate towns and villages which cling desperately to their individual identity.

Dudley may not be the largest town, but it claims to be the capital of the Black Country; with its castle it was an administrative centre from early times. There was already a castle here in Saxon times, although it was soon replaced after the Norman Conquest. It was destroyed 250 years ago as a result of a fire which no-one was prepared to risk fighting for fear of the gunpowder that was stored within, and since then it has sat as a picturesque ruin overlooking the town.

As with the rest of the region, industry has always been important in Dudley. Many of the towns have specialised in one particular product, and if Dudley could be said to have specialised it was in the production of nails, anvils and hearth furniture. One particularly sad statistic for Dudley is that in 1851 a report described the town as the unhealthiest in the country. At that time one child in every five died here before reaching the age of 12 months. This, of course, was a direct result of overcrowding, which was due to the rapidly growing population in the early 1800s. In the first 30 years of the century the Black Country's population quadrupled. New housing was built with little regard to health and sanitation, and the inevitable happened in the 1830s when the first of several serious outbreaks of cholera occurred.

Yet it was not until 1863 that the first cottage hospital was established in the area, and that was in Walsall. Walsall can claim to be just as ancient as Dudley, with a charter that dates back to the early 1200s. It was not just the hospital that was a first for Walsall – it was also one of the first towns in the country to have its own police force and social amenities such as a free library.

To this day, Walsall is associated with a very specialised industry. It is the world's saddlery capital with 65 saddlers still in production, just one of whom uses 4,500 hides a year. From the 1500s, the town was also famous for the production of other 'horsy' implements, namely buckles, spurs and stirrups. Buckles were made for shoes too, and when shoe laces were introduced in the 1790s the local people asked the Prince of Wales for his patronage to try and ensure that the new fashion would not catch on. But it did, and within 30 years the production of buckles was declining.

The town of West Bromwich close by is probably best known to most people for its football team, which began as a works team called the Strollers. By 1886 it had acquired the name 'the Albion', and the team won the FA Cup two years later. But West Bromwich has its industrial heritage too – in fact, the first recorded charcoal blast furnace in the area was built here as far back as 1590. Nearby Wednesbury was nicknamed the Tube Town. It was so-called because it was here that a local man, Cornelius Whitehouse, worked out a method of forging a hollow tube through iron in 1825.

Bilston became famous for the production of toys, but not toys as we now think of them. The people here produced enamelled ware, and their 'toys' were little enamelled boxes for wealthy and fashionable adults in the 1700s. They even produced commemorative boxes to celebrate the wedding of George III and Queen Charlotte in 1761. Many of the boxes were used to contain snuff, and the saying was that 'Bilston's snuff boxes were not to be sneezed at'.

It was locks that made Willenhall famous, some of which were extremely ornamental. At first this was largely a cottage industry, with individual families working and employing local apprentices from the workhouse. Some apprentices were so badly treated by their employers that Willenhall acquired a dubious reputation as the cruellest town in the country. Another dubious claim to fame is that of Wednesfield, for this town became famous for producing animal traps.

But it was Stourbridge and Brierley Hill, in the south, that became associated with the most beautiful products – fine quality glass. The tradition started in the early 1600s following the arrival in the area of Huguenot refugees from Europe who brought the skills with them. In recent years, Royal Brierley Crystal, the only surviving company, has been struggling for its own survival. Fortunately the company has recently received a large cash injection, and so we may hope that it will be with us for some time to come. It is now the only major company in Britain producing high quality crystal glass.

The largest town in the area, however, is Wolverhampton. Like all the other Black Country towns, it had an extensive industrial base; but perhaps for most outsiders, it was especially famous for its bicycles – in the 1890s there were 59 bicycle manufacturers in the town. I refer to it as a town, and indeed Wolverhampton only gained borough status as recently as 1848. However, in 2000 it was awarded the status of a city, thus confirming its pre-eminent position within the Black Country.

And what of the future in a region that has traditionally had its economy firmly linked to industry? Although much of the heavy industry in the Black Country has visibly declined over recent years, it has not disappeared altogether. Today industry is managing to survive in the smaller factories and the many out-of-town industrial units that have sprung up. It is, however, an unfortunate fact that unemployment in the region is high and opportunities are limited.

One surprising growth industry has been tourism. The very name 'The Black Country' has actually become the region's marketing tool. It is no longer just castles and beautiful mansions that attract visitors; instead our more recent industrial past has become an attraction in itself. Perhaps this is largely to do with the fact that so many of us can easily relate to the exhibits in museums such as the superb Black Country Museum in Dudley. Other local museums have also exploited this interest in our immediate past, and there are now museums for glass production, leather and even locks. This interest in our immediate past is also what makes the old photographs of the area that were produced by companies such as the one founded by Francis Frith of such interest to all of us.

Wolverhampton

Wolverhampton, The Market 1910 W285008
Wolverhampton has had a regular market here since
1258. This market benefited also from the
importance of the wool trade in medieval times,
giving rise to a local industry in the production of
coarse cloth. To this day there is a woolpack on the
coat of arms. The Market Hall on the right was
demolished in 1961.

◀ **Wolverhampton
St Peter's Church
c1955** W285503
Wolverhampton has just
celebrated its first
millennium, in 1985.
The first settlement on
this site was founded by
Lady Wulfruna on land
given to her by King
Aethelred in AD 985. It
also became a new city
in 2000.

◀ Wolverhampton Queen Square 1890
W285006

It is a beautiful sunny day, and the chemist has draped a sheet over one of his windows to protect the stock that is displayed behind it. In the adjacent window it is just possible to make out the wonderful shapes of some of the bottles. Notice the policeman on duty.

▶ Wolverhampton St Peter's Church c1960 W285047

The present St Peter's church dates from 1425, although it does incorporate an earlier church that stood here previously. For all that Wolverhampton is now a city, St Peter's is not a cathedral, although it was once described as certainly having 'something of the air of a cathedral'. Notice the flowerbeds in St Peter's Gardens in the foreground.

◀ Wolverhampton Market Place and St Peter's Church c1955 W285015

Known to locals as 'the Patch', the market was closed in May 1960 and this whole area has since been taken over by the new Civic Centre. Midlanders are always quick with a nickname, and the rather solid, red-brick buildings are now known as 'the Kremlin' to many people, so it is perhaps appropriate that there is even a nuclear bunker underneath the complex.

▼ **Wolverhampton, Queen Square c1960** W285048
Queen Square was once known as High Green, and served as an
open area not far from the church where markets and fairs were held.
It was renamed Queen Square following the visit of Queen Victoria to
the town in 1866.

▼ **Wolverhampton, Queen Square c1955** W285013
Queen Victoria came to unveil the statue of Prince Albert (seen here on the right).
It was the Queen's first official ceremony following her husband's death. Local
legend has it that the horse's legs are incorrect; cine film was later to prove that
horses do not walk this way. However, there are some who still argue that the
statue is correct.

▲ **Wolverhampton
Queen Square 1910**
W285002
The Empire Palace, seen
here on the left, opened
in 1898; after
refurbishment in 1921, it
was renamed the
Hippodrome. There was a
disastrous fire in 1956,
after which the site was
used by Times
Furnishings – the awful
building seen on the left
in photograph No
W285048. Today this
building, too, has been
replaced and a pub now
occupies the site.

◀ **Wolverhampton
Darlington Street 1890**
W285003
Again, it is high summer,
with all the shops on the
sunny side of the street
using their awnings. Notice,
especially, the wonderful
display of hats, mainly
summer boaters, in the
tailor's shop window on the
far right. Incidentally, the
clock is still on the building,
but it is not working these
days.

Wolverhampton, Darlington Street c1955 W285307
Darlington Street was actually opened in 1821 on land purchased from the Earl of Darlington – an indication of how the town was expanding in the early years of the 19th century. Further indication of 19th-century expansion comes from the fact that St Mark's church, seen at the end of the street, only dates from 1849.

Wolverhampton, Victoria Street c1955 W285308
The large building on the right is Beattie's department store. It was founded here in 1877 by James Beattie as the Victoria Drapery Supply Store. The building extends around the corner, but few people notice the wonderful art deco-style elephant's heads that adorn it. The buildings on the left have all been replaced by the new Mander Shopping Centre.

Wolverhampton, Victoria Street 1910 W285005
This photograph looks along the street from the other direction. This view is now totally different. The open window on the far right belongs to the oldest timber-framed building in Wolverhampton, dating from 1609. Once called Tunwall Street (the town's well was nearby) it later became Cock Street. The name was changed again following Queen Victoria's visit in 1866.

Wolverhampton, New Market Hall, School Street c1965 W285056
The new Market Hall was built in 1960 to replace the market area near St Peter's church. This street also has since been closed to traffic. There are now permanent stalls for an outdoor market where once the cars were parked.

Wolverhampton Dudley Street c1900

W285007

We love this busy street scene – notice how every single person is wearing a hat. The street has changed considerably in recent years: all the buildings on the left have been pulled down to be replaced by the Mander Centre in 1970. It was named after Benjamin Mander, who founded a japanning and varnish manufacturing company on the site in 1773.

◀ **Wolverhampton
Dudley Street c1955**
W285009
Looking back down
Dudley Street, the
building at the end has
now been replaced by
the Wulfrun Shopping
Centre. The name
Wolverhampton, or
Wulfrun Heantun as it
once was, means 'the
high farmstead
belonging to Wulfrun',
which is unusual -
Wulfruna was a lady, and
lady property-owners
were infrequent in Saxon
times.

◀ Wolverhampton Queen Street c1900

W285001

The shop in the centre, Smart & Co, has a 'Great Sale' on. Shoes are advertised for 5s 9d, 4s 9d or 3s 9d a pair. Using today's money, that is the equivalent to 29½p, 24½p or 19½p for a pair of shoes!

▼ Wolverhampton St Peter's Gardens c1955 W285305

Through the trees it is possible to see a column standing on its own: it is all that remains of an ancient Saxon preaching cross. It was once ornately carved, but it is now difficult to see the detail of the carving. It is thought to date from around AD 850.

◀ Wolverhampton St Peter's Gardens and the College of Art c1955

W285304

The fountain was erected in 1894, and it is dedicated to Philip Horsman, who presented the nearby art galley to the townspeople. The School of Art, shown here, was opened in 1885 and was granted college status in 1945. Notice the wonderful carving detail on the upper floor representing Painting, Sculpture and Science.

Wolverhampton Lichfield Street 1910

W285004

Originally known as Kem Street, this is perhaps one of the oldest streets in Wolverhampton. The car on the left being admired by the children would have still been a rare sight in 1910; the children would have been more used to the trams. We can see the tramlines along the roadway.

**Wolverhampton
Lichfield Street
c1955** W285010
The Grand Theatre (left)
opened in 1894, and
has seen performers
ranging from Ellen Terry
to Charlie Chaplin and,
more recently, Norman
Wisdom. Opposite was
the Co-op (there is a
Co-op van parked
outside). Today the
building has become a
Weatherspoons pub.
Buildings further up the
street are now nearly all
occupied by the
University of
Wolverhampton.

◄ **Wolverhampton Lichfield Street and the Art Gallery c1955**
W285012
When the Art Gallery was opened in 1884 by Lord Wrottesley, he used a golden key that had been made by the local firm of Chubb and Sons Lock and Safe Co Ltd. Although originally a London firm, Chubbs had opened its first factory in the town in 1818.

Wolverhampton, Lichfield Street c1955 W285011

The junction in the foreground is known as Princes Square, and in 1927 it was the site of the very first set of traffic lights in the country. The experiment carried out here proved to be so successful (!) that from the following year traffic lights were introduced throughout Great Britain.

▼ Wolverhampton, Molineaux Football Ground c1960

W285035

This is the home of the Wolves (or Wolverhampton Wanderers Football Club); a superb new stadium has now replaced this one. The club was founded in 1887. It was one of the original twelve members of the Football League, winning the FA Cup for the first time in 1893.

◄ Wolverhampton, West Park c1960 W285044

The West Park was opened in 1881. Originally the land was known as Broad Meadow, and was used as the town's racecourse. The Conservatory, shown here, was opened in 1896. Overlooking this boating lake stands a statue for a former MP for Wolverhampton: Charles Pelham Villiers was Wolverhampton's MP for over 60 years, yet never once even visited the town!

▼ **Wolverhampton, The Clock, West Park c1965** W285058
Altogether Wolverhampton has around 200 acres of parkland, and West Park is
the finest. The clock, now painted blue, was presented to the town by Councillor
J Ross in 1883. Notice the beautiful display of roses – Floral Fetes used to be
held here (the first took place in 1889), and regularly drew in between 90,000
and 100,000 people.

▼ **Wolverhampton, The Grammar School, Compton Road c1960** W285038
Like many schools around the country, Wolverhampton Grammar School
was founded in the 16th century, in this case by Sir Stephen Jenys, who was
Lord Mayor of London in 1508. Originally it stood where the Mander Centre
now stands in the heart of the town, and it moved to this site in 1874.

▲ **Wolverhampton
Chapel Ash c1955**
W285302
Today Chapel Ash is a
busy junction leading
towards Shropshire and
the west. Originally, this
would have been a totally
separate settlement
beyond the town's limits.
The poet Alfred Noyes,
who wrote the 'Song of
England', was born in
Chapel Ash in 1880.

◀ **Wolverhampton Royal Wolverhampton School c1955** W285030
Royal Wolverhampton School is a much later foundation. Originally it was the Royal Orphanage Asylum, founded by John Lees, a wealthy local merchant, to care for children whose parents had been killed in a recent cholera epidemic. The main building cost £38,000 to build, and was enlarged as early as 1865 at an additional cost of £46,000.

◄ **Wolverhampton East Park c1955**

W285019

Like the West Park on the other side of the town, the East Park is around 50 acres in size. Parks with numerous individual flower beds, as depicted here, are very labour intensive – notice the gardener's wheelbarrow – and are seen less and less today.

**Wolverhampton
Royal Wolverhampton
School c1955** W285031
In 1944 the Royal
Orphanage Asylum changed
its name to become the
Royal Wolverhampton
School. Perhaps its most
famous old boy was Gilbert
Harding. He was to achieve
fame in the early days of
television as a popular
panellist on game shows
such as 'What's My Line?'

**Wolverhampton
East Park c1955**
W285016
The presence of parks
was considered an
essential asset for
communities where
populations had
exploded during the
Industrial Revolution,
with the subsequent
development of factories
and back-to-back
housing. In
Wolverhampton, for
example, the population
soared from 12,500 in
1801 to 95,000 a
century later.

Around Wolverhampton

Penn, Spring Hill Corner c1965 P157026
The style of the windows in the white building in the centre of this photograph tells us that this parade of shops dates from the 1930s. In fact they were built in 1935.

Penn, The Village c1965 P157022
Perhaps the original village of Penn predates its many neighbours – the name of the village comes from an old Celtic word meaning 'the place at the hill'. Also, the church nearby has a base for an ancient medieval cross, which is said to have been set up by Lady Godiva. The pub on the corner here is the Fox and Goose.

Wolverhampton, Penn Common c1955 W285020
Penn Common was once part of the Royal Forest of Kinver - in other words, it was a hunting ground. The word 'forest' in Norman times did not necessarily mean a wooded area; such hunting grounds were often open areas where deer could roam unmolested.

Wolverhampton, Penn Common c1955 W285021
There have been many disputes over the use and ownership of the common. In the 19th century bare-fisted fights were held here – these were illegal in Wolverhampton, but the common was close enough to the town for locals to come and watch the fights and gamble on the outcome. Today there is a golf club here which was founded in 1892.

Wombourn, Bratch Locks c1965 W323009 The Staffordshire and Worcestershire Canal, built by James Brindley, was opened in 1772. The 46-mile canal cost over £100,000. The Bratch Locks just outside Wombourn was originally a three-lock staircase allowing the canal to rise 30ft. The pretty little octagonal building with its central chimney at the top was the toll house, now no longer painted white.

▼ Wombourn, Gravel Hill c1965 W323022

The sign tells us that this was the Seisdon Rural District Council. Today it houses the Wombourn Civic Centre. Modern buildings often seem to consist mainly of glass. Wombourn's church is dedicated to St Benedict Biscop, who is said to have introduced glass windows to England.

▼ Seisdon, The Stores c1960
S797307D

This building still houses the village post office and stores, but the petrol station has now gone. If we enlarge the image, we can see from the petrol pumps that petrol then cost 6s 1d (30p) for a gallon of Supreme and 5s 7d (28p) for a gallon of the Regular.

▲ Tettenhall, The Parish Church c1960 T140013A

Most of the present church was rebuilt after a fire in 1950, which was said by some to have been started by a choir boy smoking! Another local story is that once an old lady insisted on sitting within the hollow yew tree to knit on a Sunday. Her arms dropped off and she was turned to stone! The tree is still there, but I can't find the stone.

Patshull, Patshull Hall 1898 41871
Built in the 18th century, Patshull overlooks beautiful countryside, far removed from reminders of the Black Country nearby. The gardens were designed by Capability Brown, who created an enormous lake in 1768. Much of the estate has since been developed as a hotel with an 18-hole golf course. The hotel's reception area includes an old folly, a Grecian temple built in 1754.

Tettenhall, The Clock Tower c1960 T140005

'I labour here with all my might to tell the hours by day and night'. Overlooking the main road, this clock was donated by Mr and Mrs Edward Swindley to the Urban District of Tettenhall in June 1911 to commemorate King George V's coronation.

Tettenhall, The Post Office and Upper Green c1965 T140012
The village of Tettenhall surrounds a really large village green which, fortunately, still survives today. This means that although Tettenhall is part of the urbanised area that surrounds Wolverhampton, it retains a feeling that it is more of a village. Notice, in this photograph, the weighing machine on the pavement.

Essington, Hobnock Road c1965 E191019
Local legend has it that 'Hob' was an old word for the Devil, and that this was therefore once the Devil's Road. Why this should be so no-one today seems to know.

Essington, The Signal Box c1965 E191015
The signal box overlooked a railway line (seen here on the left) that connected with local coal mines; it was not a main line. Today there is a garden where the trains once travelled, and the building, since enlarged, is now used as a craft shop.

Wednesfield, High Street c1965 W236015
Wednesfield means 'the open land of Woden', a heathen god. Although there has been a settlement here since time immemorial, the first chapel, dedicated to St Thomas, was not built until 1750. It became a proper church after Wednesfield achieved parish status in 1841. Most of the present church of St Thomas was rebuilt after a fire in 1902.

**Wednesfield
The Canal and the Flats c1965**
W236013
In recent years Wednesfield has developed very much as a dormitory town serving Wolverhampton – in the 1950s alone the population of the parish nearly doubled – and the blocks of flats seen here are typical of many that were built throughout the Birmingham area during the 1950s and 1960s.

**Willenhall
The Clock Tower c1960**
W238018A
This extremely ornate clock (notice the wonderful ironwork detail) and drinking fountain was built as a memorial to a local doctor, Dr Joseph Tonks. It was erected in 1892, and was then restored in 1979.

Willenhall, Ye Olde Toll House c1965 W238014
Willenhall was particularly famous for the production of locks. This was a skilled task, and workers soon became permanently stooped from leaning over their workbenches. Willenhall was therefore known as 'Umpshire', and legend has it that some pubs even had holes cut into the walls behind their benches so that the humpbacked men could sit and drink comfortably!

Walsall to West Bromwich

Walsall
The Bridge 1908 W161001
Not so much a bridge, more a large open square, The Bridge is
so-named because it was under here that a tributary of the River
Tame once flowed; it was culverted over many years ago. As it
carried much of the town's effluent, there are still people in the
town who remember how it used to smell in the summer time.

Walsall ▶
The Bridge c1965
W161032X
Here we see the first
statue of a non-royal lady
in England: Sister Dora,
who wanted to join
Florence Nightingale in
the Crimea. As her father
disapproved she came to
Walsall instead, and
worked at the local
cottage hospital until her
death from cancer in
1878. The original statue
was made of white
marble, but it became so
badly affected by
pollution that there is
now a bronze replica.

▼ Wednesbury, St Paul's Church c1965 W235003
It is said that there was once a temple to the pagan god, Woden, near here. Today,
instead, a stained glass window in the church reads 'In grateful commemoration of
the overthrow of a heathen religion, especially the worship of a false god, Woden,
and the establishment of the worship of the True God by the inhabitants of
Wednesbury'.

**▲ Walsall, Park Street
1967** W161018
Today the symbol
associated with Lloyds
Bank is a black horse; we
can see a small black
horse on the corner of
the bank building. Above
it, however, is the original
symbol of the bank – a
beautifully-carved beehive
symbolising thrift and
industry.

◀ **Wednesbury, High Street c1960** W235012
The town was once described as a 'dark, dirty, mean-looking place where the local people scarcely ever thought of anything but eating and drinking when the day's labour is done'. The clock shown here was erected to commemorate the coronation of King George V in 1911; it has four illuminated clock faces.

West Bromwich, High Street 1963 W237016
This town was once described as a 'bald and ugly place'! People, even the locals, seem to have always been very complimentary about the Black Country! The tall building pictured is the Town Hall, and its tower is 130 ft high. Next door is the library which opened in 1907, thanks largely to a donation from Andrew Carnegie.

Bilston, The Greyhound Inn c1960 B353005
The Greyhound stands in the High Street in Bilston, and it is a remarkable survival in an area where, by and large, few ancient buildings survive. It dates from 1458, and was restored in the 1930s by the brewers, William Butler and Co. These days it is known as the Greyhound and Punchbowl.

Bilston, St Leonard's Church c1960 B353023
The tower of St Leonard's church originally had four pinnacles on the top. When the church was restored in 1733, they were removed at a cost of £31. The 'father of the South Staffordshire iron trade' was born in Bilston in 1728. His name was John Wilkinson, and when he died he was buried in an iron coffin.

Bilston, Lichfield Street c1960 B353004 The building behind the trees is the Town Hall. One of its signs advertises a dance with a band called 'The In Betweens', and the other advertises the availability of improvement grants. The building was constructed in 1872. It stands on old pit workings (a common problem with buildings all over the Black Country), and so in 1906 its foundations needed to be strengthened.

Sedgley, The Bull Ring 1968 S336012
Places called 'the Bull Ring' are often assumed to be sites where bull-baiting took place, but it might simply have been used for a cattle market. This scene has changed little - even the roundabout has managed to survive.

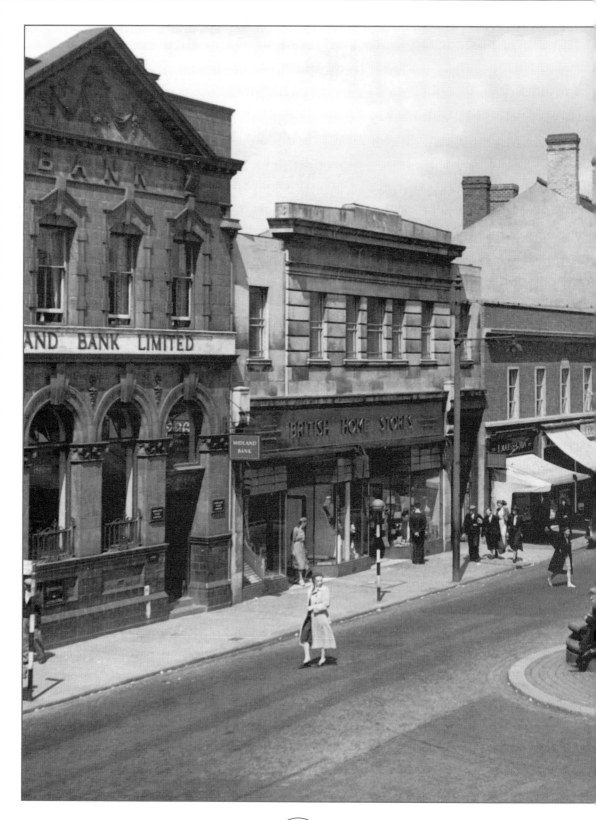

Dudley to Stourbridge

**Dudley, The Market Place
c1955** D103028
This magnificent fountain was displayed at the Paris Exhibition in 1867 before being erected here; it was known locally as 'the spout'. A new statue faces it now – Duncan Edwards was born in Dudley. He could have become one of England's finest footballers, but he died in the Munich air tragedy in 1958.

◀ **Dudley
Castle Hill 1968**

D103192

It is interesting to compare the left-hand side of the street with its new row of shops with the earlier photograph (number D103026) taken around 15 years before. All the buildings have changed. Included in these shops is a branch of Fine Fare, an early supermarket. Dudley Castle can be seen on the hillside overlooking the town.

◄ Dudley, Castle Street and St Edmund's Church c1955

D103026

Although there has been a church on this site since Saxon times, the present church replaces one that was destroyed during the Civil War in the 17th century. Royalist defenders in the castle on the hill behind deliberately demolished it for fear that the Roundhead soldiers might use it as a base from which to attack the castle.

◄ Dudley The Castle Keep c1955 D103049A

Queen Elizabeth visited the castle in 1575, but some years later, when plans were mooted for it to become a prison for Mary, Queen of Scots, a report so condemned the place that she was imprisoned elsewhere. This was probably a politically-motivated decision by a Dudley who wanted to avoid any risks associated with Mary's future.

Dudley ► The Castle Gateway 1949 D103004

The statue is that of the second Earl of Dudley, and was erected in 1888. His family can trace their links with the area back to the 1500s, when John Dudley took over the castle here. John Dudley became the Duke of Northumberland, tried to set his niece, Lady Jane Grey, on the throne of England and was later executed by Mary Tudor.

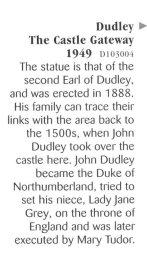

▼ **Dudley, Dudley Zoo, The Lion Enclosure c1965** D103156
Dudley Zoo sits on a 40-acre site in the former grounds of the castle, and
was opened in 1937. At that time it was considered extremely modern
because it gave the animals so much space; but zoos are no longer so
fashionable, and it is now struggling for its very survival. The enclosure
shown here is now used for tigers.

▼ **Dudley, Dudley Zoo, The Elephants c1965** D103255
Notice the chain being used to tether the elephant in the foreground.
Present-day staff at the zoo were horrified to see this. It would certainly
never be done these days.

▲ **Kingswinford
The Townsend Precinct
c1965** K84009
This shopping precinct
sits in the centre of
Kingswinford overlooking
a very busy road junction.
It must have been
considered extremely
futuristic when it was first
built in the 1960s shortly
before this photograph
was taken.

◄ **Wordsley, New Housing c1965** W240047
The new houses here are a reminder of the constant development in the area. It was Wordsley that provided the pub for the Black Country Museum – the Bottle and Glass. There is a local joke that in World War II many bombs fell on pubs: there were so many pubs around that it was difficult for the Luftwaffe to miss them.

Brierley Hill, The View from Amblecote Road c1965 B355002
This is a general view of Brierley Hill looking from the south-east; it gives a good impression of the hilltop site the settlement occupied. In fact, the row of tower blocks is a landmark from all directions. The tower of St Michael's church can just be distinguished on the skyline in the middle of all the modern buildings.

Brierley Hill, St Michael's Church c1965 B355007
Built in 1765 on the highest ground in the parish, St Michael's church was then the main landmark here. It was enlarged in 1823 and again in 1837, a sure indication of the growth of the local population at that time. It is typical of many Georgian churches in its design, and is only immediately recognisable as a church because of its tower, which was rebuilt in 1900.

Brierley Hill, West Midlands Constabulary c1965 B355014
Brierley Hill's police station originally stood in the High Street before it moved to its present site. The police station occupies the building on the left in this photograph. The building on the right is Brierley Hill's Civic Hall.

Brierley Hill, The Canal Locks c1965 B355004
There is not just one lock here: behind the first lock it is possible to make out a whole flight of locks. Although known as the Nine Locks, there are actually only eight locks here: the flight was rebuilt in 1857, and one lock was then removed. A pub half-way along the flight came to be known as the Tenth Lock.

**Brierley Hill
High Street c1965**
B355017
The main street in
Brierley Hill is much the
same today. The
entrance to the indoor
market can just be seen
behind the lamppost on
the left of the street.

Lye, High Street c1965 L178004
In the early 19th century, Lye was called the 'mud city' because there were so many buildings in the village that were constructed of the local clay. Today they seem to have all been replaced by brick. By the 1860s there were over 100 companies producing bricks locally. Notice the parked car with the collection of badges along its radiator grill.

Stourbridge, The Mitre Inn c1960 S213057
Stourbridge has been altered considerably over recent years with the building of a ring road all around the heart of the town. Fortunately, that heart still beats, and much of the town is easily recognisable in these photographs, although the gardens in this picture have gone.

Stourbridge, The Grammar School c1965 S213176
The King Edward VI School was founded in 1552, and so celebrates its 450th anniversary in 2002. Nikolaus Pevsner described the tower as 'picturesque', but I particularly admire the 1930s extension with its superb carving detail which we can see on the right of the photograph here.

▼ **Stourbridge, Lower High Street c1965** S213162
Notice the town clock standing beyond the road junction. It was constructed in
1857 at John Bradley's Ironworks, a local company sited near the Stourbridge
Canal. Today it serves as a useful meeting point beside the new shopping
centre, the Crown Centre, the entrance to which is just to the right.

▼ **Stourbridge, St Thomas' Church, Market Street c1965** S213164
The large sign outside the church is announcing an appeal for the restoration of the
church tower and its bells. £5,000 was needed, and by the time this photograph
was taken £3,800 had been raised. It would appear that all the money was raised -
certainly the brickwork for the tower has since been repointed. The building on the
left is the church hall, which dates from 1914.

▲ **Stourbridge, Market
Street c1965** S213160
Few of the buildings in
this street have been
altered in the intervening
years. The modern
building on the left is the
Institute and Social Club,
and beyond it the tall
building (which dates
from 1887) houses
Stourbridge's Theatre.

◀ **Stourbridge, High Street c1965** S213161
Compare the building with the arched façade (now Paperway Stationers) with photograph No 84687 – we are looking along the street from the opposite direction. The 1960s replacement for the upper floors may give more space internally, but it is not in the least bit pleasing to look at.

Dudley to Stourbridge

**Stourbridge
The High Street 1931**
84687
This is a wonderfully evocative view that would be typical of any town in 1930s England. I particularly like the row of parked cars. Notice, also, the window cleaners, and the ladies with their cloche-style hats walking quite unconcernedly below them!

Stourbridge, High Street c1960 S213054
All the buildings behind the cars have been demolished to make way for a new ring road around the centre of Stourbridge. The road was, and still is, much criticised by local people because of the way in which it almost totally isolated the town centre within a Grand Prix-like circuit of roads.

Stourbridge, High Street c1960 S213052
It is the foreground area of this photograph that has been totally obliterated to make way for the ring road. This means that the High Street now comes to a virtual dead end where the pedestrian crossing can be seen.

Stourbridge, The War Memorial c1965 S213137
The war memorial was designed by Ernest W Pickford, and was unveiled by the Earl of Coventry in 1923. When the New Road, as the ring road is actually called at this point, was built the memorial itself was saved; it now stands in Mary Stevens Park on the edge of the town.

Stourbridge, The Public Library c1965 S213136
The former public library is the red-brick building in the centre. Like the library in West Bromwich, it was erected thanks largely to the generosity of Andrew Carnegie. The clock tower on the right was a later addition built in memory of Isaac Nash, an edge-tool manufacturer.

▼ **Stourbridge, Hagley Road c1965** S213154
This is now a very busy road junction leading into Stourbridge from
the south. The pub on the right, the Cross Inn, still survives, and has
a rather fine pub sign in the form of a metal cross.

▼ **Old Swinford, St Mary's Church c1965** S213147
There are a number of churches that serve the people who live in Stourbridge.
St Mary's could be described as the mother church, as there has been a church
on this site since at least the 13th century. Today St Mary's church in Old Swinford
is no longer the landmark that it once was, since the steeple has gone.

▲ **Old Swinford
General View c1965**
051146
Today the main town here
is Stourbridge, but
originally it was Swinford,
on the higher ground,
that was the more
important settlement.
Then some people
moved to settle beside
the crossing of the River
Stour, and already by the
14th century Stourbridge
had outgrown its parent.

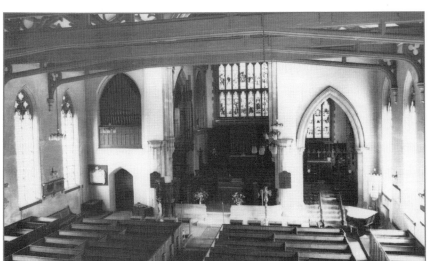

◄ **Old Swinford, St Mary's Church, The Interior c1965** S213149
Most of the present church (apart from the 14th-century tower, which survives) was rebuilt in the 1800s, and some of it was then restored once again in 1938.

◀ **Stourbridge
Worcester Lane
Pedmore c1965**

S213153
Little has changed here
in the intervening years,
except that the road is
much busier and the
trees are taller. One
thing has gone, though –
the steeple of St Mary's
at Old Swinford in the
background.

◄ **Stourbridge
Old Swinford
Hospital School for
Boys c1955** S213016
Despite the name
'hospital', this was
originally a charity
school set up in the 17th
century by Thomas
Foley for 60 poor boys.
They were destined to
become local
apprentices once they
had completed their
education here.

▼ **Stourbridge
The Entrance Gates to
Mary Stevens Park 1931**
84693
These magnificent gates
mark the entrance to Heath
House, once the home of
Ernest Stevens. He was a
millionaire who made his
fortune as a manufacturer of
hollow-ware, which is
hollow metal ware such as
cups and saucepans.

◄ **Stourbridge
Mary Stevens Park
c1955** S213048
Ernest Stevens was
Stourbridge's greatest
public benefactor.
Having made his fortune,
some of it as a result of
supplying the British
army with billy-cans,
cutlery and so on, in
1929 he presented this
estate to the town. It was
then formally opened by
him in April 1931.

Stourbridge, The Council Buildings and the Bowling Green c1955 S213021
The estate is now known as Mary Stevens Park in memory of Ernest Stevens' wife. The buildings shown here include the 18th-century mansion that was previously known as Heath House, along with the modern office buildings that were added when it was converted into the Council Offices for the town.

Stourbridge, The Lake, Mary Stevens Park 1931 84697
It is tranquil parks such as this that help to bring the 'green borderland' described by Elihu Burritt in 1868 right into the 'black country' to the benefit of all who live here. Altogether this park covers an area of about 30 acres.

Index

Bilston 54, 55, 56-57

Bratch Locks 42-43

Brierley Hill 66, 67, 68-69

Chapel Ash 34-35

Dudley 60-61, 62-63

Dudley Zoo 64

Essington 47, 48

Kingswinford 64-65

Lye 70

Old Swinford 78-79, 80-81

Patshull 44-45

Pedmore 80

Penn 38-39, 40

Penn Common 40, 41

Sedgley 58-59

Seisdon 44

Stourbridge 70, 71, 72-73, 74-75,
    76, 77, 78, 80-81, 82

Tettenhall 44, 46, 47

Walsall 51, 52-53

Wednesbury 52, 53

Wednesfield 49

West Bromwich 54

Willenhall 50

Wolverhampton 16-17, 18-19, 20-21,
    22, 23, 24-25, 26-27, 28-29,
    30-31, 32-33, 34-35, 36-37

Wombourn 42-43, 44

Wordsley 65

Frith Book Co Titles

www.francisfrith.co.uk

The Frith Book Company publishes over 100 new titles each year. A selection of those currently available are listed below. For latest catalogue please contact Frith Book Co.

Town Books 96 pages, approx 100 photos. County and Themed Books 128 pages, approx 150 photos (unless specified). All titles hardback laminated case and jacket except those indicated pb (paperback)

Title	ISBN	Price
Amersham, Chesham & Rickmansworth (pb)	1-85937-340-2	£9.99
Ancient Monuments & Stone Circles	1-85937-143-4	£17.99
Aylesbury (pb)	1-85937-227-9	£9.99
Bakewell	1-85937-113-2	£12.99
Barnstaple (pb)	1-85937-300-3	£9.99
Bath (pb)	1-85937419-0	£9.99
Bedford (pb)	1-85937-205-8	£9.99
Berkshire (pb)	1-85937-191-4	£9.99
Berkshire Churches	1-85937-170-1	£17.99
Blackpool (pb)	1-85937-382-8	£9.99
Bognor Regis (pb)	1-85937-431-x	£9.99
Bournemouth	1-85937-067-5	£12.99
Bradford (pb)	1-85937-204-x	£9.99
Brighton & Hove(pb)	1-85937-192-2	£8.99
Bristol (pb)	1-85937-264-3	£9.99
British Life A Century Ago (pb)	1-85937-213-9	£9.99
Buckinghamshire (pb)	1-85937-200-7	£9.99
Camberley (pb)	1-85937-222-8	£9.99
Cambridge (pb)	1-85937-422-0	£9.99
Cambridgeshire (pb)	1-85937-420-4	£9.99
Canals & Waterways (pb)	1-85937-291-0	£9.99
Canterbury Cathedral (pb)	1-85937-179-5	£9.99
Cardiff (pb)	1-85937-093-4	£9.99
Carmarthenshire	1-85937-216-3	£14.99
Chelmsford (pb)	1-85937-310-0	£9.99
Cheltenham (pb)	1-85937-095-0	£9.99
Cheshire (pb)	1-85937-271-6	£9.99
Chester	1-85937-090-x	£12.99
Chesterfield	1-85937-378-x	£9.99
Chichester (pb)	1-85937-228-7	£9.99
Colchester (pb)	1-85937-188-4	£8.99
Cornish Coast	1-85937-163-9	£14.99
Cornwall (pb)	1-85937-229-5	£9.99
Cornwall Living Memories	1-85937-248-1	£14.99
Cotswolds (pb)	1-85937-230-9	£9.99
Cotswolds Living Memories	1-85937-255-4	£14.99
County Durham	1-85937-123-x	£14.99
Croydon Living Memories	1-85937-162-0	£9.99
Cumbria	1-85937-101-9	£14.99
Dartmoor	1-85937-145-0	£14.99
Derby (pb)	1-85937-367-4	£9.99
Derbyshire (pb)	1-85937-196-5	£9.99
Devon (pb)	1-85937-297-x	£9.99
Dorset (pb)	1-85937-269-4	£9.99
Dorset Churches	1-85937-172-8	£17.99
Dorset Coast (pb)	1-85937-299-6	£9.99
Dorset Living Memories	1-85937-210-4	£14.99
Down the Severn	1-85937-118-3	£14.99
Down the Thames (pb)	1-85937-278-3	£9.99
Down the Trent	1-85937-311-9	£14.99
Dublin (pb)	1-85937-231-7	£9.99
East Anglia (pb)	1-85937-265-1	£9.99
East London	1-85937-080-2	£14.99
East Sussex	1-85937-130-2	£14.99
Eastbourne	1-85937-061-6	£12.99
Edinburgh (pb)	1-85937-193-0	£8.99
England in the 1880s	1-85937-331-3	£17.99
English Castles (pb)	1-85937-434-4	£9.99
English Country Houses	1-85937-161-2	£17.99
Essex (pb)	1-85937-270-8	£9.99
Exeter	1-85937-126-4	£12.99
Exmoor	1-85937-132-9	£14.99
Falmouth	1-85937-066-7	£12.99
Folkestone (pb)	1-85937-124-8	£9.99
Glasgow (pb)	1-85937-190-6	£9.99
Gloucestershire	1-85937-102-7	£14.99
Great Yarmouth (pb)	1-85937-426-3	£9.99
Greater Manchester (pb)	1-85937-266-x	£9.99
Guildford (pb)	1-85937-410-7	£9.99
Hampshire (pb)	1-85937-279-1	£9.99
Hampshire Churches (pb)	1-85937-207-4	£9.99
Harrogate	1-85937-423-9	£9.99
Hastings & Bexhill (pb)	1-85937-131-0	£9.99
Heart of Lancashire (pb)	1-85937-197-3	£9.99
Helston (pb)	1-85937-214-7	£9.99
Hereford (pb)	1-85937-175-2	£9.99
Herefordshire	1-85937-174-4	£14.99
Hertfordshire (pb)	1-85937-247-3	£9.99
Horsham (pb)	1-85937-432-8	£9.99
Humberside	1-85937-215-5	£14.99
Hythe, Romney Marsh & Ashford	1-85937-256-2	£9.99

Available from your local bookshop or from the publisher

Frith Book Co Titles (continued)

Title	ISBN	Price	Title	ISBN	Price
Ipswich (pb)	1-85937-424-7	£9.99	St Ives (pb)	1-85937415-8	£9.99
Ireland (pb)	1-85937-181-7	£9.99	Scotland (pb)	1-85937-182-5	£9.99
Isle of Man (pb)	1-85937-268-6	£9.99	Scottish Castles (pb)	1-85937-323-2	£9.99
Isles of Scilly	1-85937-136-1	£14.99	Sevenoaks & Tunbridge	1-85937-057-8	£12.99
Isle of Wight (pb)	1-85937-429-8	£9.99	Sheffield, South Yorks (pb)	1-85937-267-8	£9.99
Isle of Wight Living Memories	1-85937-304-6	£14.99	Shrewsbury (pb)	1-85937-325-9	£9.99
Kent (pb)	1-85937-189-2	£9.99	Shropshire (pb)	1-85937-326-7	£9.99
Kent Living Memories	1-85937-125-6	£14.99	Somerset	1-85937-153-1	£14.99
Lake District (pb)	1-85937-275-9	£9.99	South Devon Coast	1-85937-107-8	£14.99
Lancaster, Morecambe & Heysham (pb)	1-85937-233-3	£9.99	South Devon Living Memories	1-85937-168-x	£14.99
Leeds (pb)	1-85937-202-3	£9.99	South Hams	1-85937-220-1	£14.99
Leicester	1-85937-073-x	£12.99	Southampton (pb)	1-85937-427-1	£9.99
Leicestershire (pb)	1-85937-185-x	£9.99	Southport (pb)	1-85937-425-5	£9.99
Lincolnshire (pb)	1-85937-433-6	£9.99	Staffordshire	1-85937-047-0	£12.99
Liverpool & Merseyside (pb)	1-85937-234-1	£9.99	Stratford upon Avon	1-85937-098-5	£12.99
London (pb)	1-85937-183-3	£9.99	Suffolk (pb)	1-85937-221-x	£9.99
Ludlow (pb)	1-85937-176-0	£9.99	Suffolk Coast	1-85937-259-7	£14.99
Luton (pb)	1-85937-235-x	£9.99	Surrey (pb)	1-85937-240-6	£9.99
Maidstone	1-85937-056-x	£14.99	Sussex (pb)	1-85937-184-1	£9.99
Manchester (pb)	1-85937-198-1	£9.99	Swansea (pb)	1-85937-167-1	£9.99
Middlesex	1-85937-158-2	£14.99	Tees Valley & Cleveland	1-85937-211-2	£14.99
New Forest	1-85937-128-0	£14.99	Thanet (pb)	1-85937-116-7	£9.99
Newark (pb)	1-85937-366-6	£9.99	Tiverton (pb)	1-85937-178-7	£9.99
Newport, Wales (pb)	1-85937-258-9	£9.99	Torbay	1-85937-063-2	£12.99
Newquay (pb)	1-85937-421-2	£9.99	Truro	1-85937-147-7	£12.99
Norfolk (pb)	1-85937-195-7	£9.99	Victorian and Edwardian Cornwall	1-85937-252-x	£14.99
Norfolk Living Memories	1-85937-217-1	£14.99	Victorian & Edwardian Devon	1-85937-253-8	£14.99
Northamptonshire	1-85937-150-7	£14.99	Victorian & Edwardian Kent	1-85937-149-3	£14.99
Northumberland Tyne & Wear (pb)	1-85937-281-3	£9.99	Vic & Ed Maritime Album	1-85937-144-2	£17.99
North Devon Coast	1-85937-146-9	£14.99	Victorian and Edwardian Sussex	1-85937-157-4	£14.99
North Devon Living Memories	1-85937-261-9	£14.99	Victorian & Edwardian Yorkshire	1-85937-154-x	£14.99
North London	1-85937-206-6	£14.99	Victorian Seaside	1-85937-159-0	£17.99
North Wales (pb)	1-85937-298-8	£9.99	Villages of Devon (pb)	1-85937-293-7	£9.99
North Yorkshire (pb)	1-85937-236-8	£9.99	Villages of Kent (pb)	1-85937-294-5	£9.99
Norwich (pb)	1-85937-194-9	£8.99	Villages of Sussex (pb)	1-85937-295-3	£9.99
Nottingham (pb)	1-85937-324-0	£9.99	Warwickshire (pb)	1-85937-203-1	£9.99
Nottinghamshire (pb)	1-85937-187-6	£9.99	Welsh Castles (pb)	1-85937-322-4	£9.99
Oxford (pb)	1-85937-411-5	£9.99	West Midlands (pb)	1-85937-289-9	£9.99
Oxfordshire (pb)	1-85937-430-1	£9.99	West Sussex	1-85937-148-5	£14.99
Peak District (pb)	1-85937-280-5	£9.99	West Yorkshire (pb)	1-85937-201-5	£9.99
Penzance	1-85937-069-1	£12.99	Weymouth (pb)	1-85937-209-0	£9.99
Peterborough (pb)	1-85937-219-8	£9.99	Wiltshire (pb)	1-85937-277-5	£9.99
Piers	1-85937-237-6	£17.99	Wiltshire Churches (pb)	1-85937-171-x	£9.99
Plymouth	1-85937-119-1	£12.99	Wiltshire Living Memories	1-85937-245-7	£14.99
Poole & Sandbanks (pb)	1-85937-251-1	£9.99	Winchester (pb)	1-85937-428-x	£9.99
Preston (pb)	1-85937-212-0	£9.99	Windmills & Watermills	1-85937-242-2	£17.99
Reading (pb)	1-85937-238-4	£9.99	Worcester (pb)	1-85937-165-5	£9.99
Romford (pb)	1-85937-319-4	£9.99	Worcestershire	1-85937-152-3	£14.99
Salisbury (pb)	1-85937-239-2	£9.99	York (pb)	1-85937-199-x	£9.99
Scarborough (pb)	1-85937-379-8	£9.99	Yorkshire (pb)	1-85937-186-8	£9.99
St Albans (pb)	1-85937-341-0	£9.99	Yorkshire Living Memories	1-85937-166-3	£14.99

See Frith books on the internet www.francisfrith.co.uk

FRITH PRODUCTS & SERVICES

Francis Frith would doubtless be pleased to know that the pioneering publishing venture he started in 1860 still continues today. A hundred and forty years later, The Francis Frith Collection continues in the same innovative tradition and is now one of the foremost publishers of vintage photographs in the world. Some of the current activities include:

Interior Decoration

Today Frith's photographs can be seen framed and as giant wall murals in thousands of pubs, restaurants, hotels, banks, retail stores and other public buildings throughout the country. In every case they enhance the unique local atmosphere of the places they depict and provide reminders of gentler days in an increasingly busy and frenetic world.

Product Promotions

Frith products are used by many major companies to promote the sales of their own products or to reinforce their own history and heritage. Frith promotions have been used by Hovis bread, Courage beers, Scots Porage Oats, Colman's mustard, Cadbury's foods, Mellow Birds coffee, Dunhill pipe tobacco, Guinness, and Bulmer's Cider.

Genealogy and Family History

As the interest in family history and roots grows world-wide, more and more people are turning to Frith's photographs of Great Britain for images of the towns, villages and streets where their ancestors lived; and, of course, photographs of the churches and chapels where their ancestors were christened, married and buried are an essential part of every genealogy tree and family album.

Frith Products

All Frith photographs are available Framed or just as Mounted Prints and Posters (size 23 x 16 inches). These may be ordered from the address below. From time to time other products - Address Books, Calendars, Table Mats, etc - are available.

The Internet

Already twenty thousand Frith photographs can be viewed and purchased on the internet through the Frith websites and a myriad of partner sites.

For more detailed information on Frith companies and products, look at these sites:

www.francisfrith.co.uk
www.francisfrith.com
(for North American visitors)

See the complete list of Frith Books at:

www.francisfrith.co.uk

This web site is regularly updated with the latest list of publications from the Frith Book Company. If you wish to buy books relating to another part of the country that your local bookshop does not stock, you may purchase on-line.

For further information, trade, or author enquiries please contact us at the address below:
The Francis Frith Collection, Frith's Barn, Teffont, Salisbury, Wiltshire, England SP3 5QP.
Tel: +44 (0)1722 716 376 Fax: +44 (0)1722 716 881 Email: sales@francisfrith.co.uk

See Frith books on the internet www.francisfrith.co.uk

TO RECEIVE YOUR FREE MOUNTED PRINT

Mounted Print
Overall size 14 x 11 inches

Cut out this Voucher and return it with your remittance for £1.95 to cover postage and handling, to UK addresses. For overseas addresses please include £4.00 post and handling. Choose any photograph included in this book. Your SEPIA print will be A4 in size, and mounted in a cream mount with burgundy rule line, overall size 14 x 11 inches.

Order additional Mounted Prints at HALF PRICE (only £7.49 each*)

If there are further pictures you would like to order, possibly as gifts for friends and family, purchase them at half price (no additional postage and handling required).

Have your Mounted Prints framed*

For an additional £14.95 per print you can have your chosen Mounted Print framed in an elegant polished wood and gilt moulding, overall size 16 x 13 inches (no additional postage and handling required).

---

* IMPORTANT!
These special prices are only available if ordered using the original voucher on this page (no copies permitted) and at the same time as your free Mounted Print, for delivery to the same address

---

Frith Collectors' Guild

From time to time we publish a magazine of news and stories about Frith photographs and further special offers of Frith products. If you would like 12 months FREE membership, please return this form.

Send completed forms to:
The Francis Frith Collection, Frith's Barn, Teffont, Salisbury, Wiltshire SP3 5QP

Voucher for FREE and Reduced Price Frith Prints

Picture no.	Page number	Qty	Mounted @ £7.49	Framed + £14.95	Total Cost
		1	**Free of charge***	£	£
			£7.49	£	£
			£7.49	£	£
			£7.49	£	£
			£7.49	£	£
			£7.49	£	£

Please allow 28 days for delivery *** Post & handling** **£1.95**

Book Title . . . . **Total Order Cost** **£**

Please do not photocopy this voucher. Only the original is valid, so please cut it out and return it to us.

I enclose a cheque / postal order for £ . . . .
made payable to 'The Francis Frith Collection'
OR please debit my Mastercard / Visa / Switch / Amex card
(credit cards please on all overseas orders)

Number . . . .

Issue No(Switch only) . . . . .Valid from (Amex/Switch) . . . .

Expires . . . .   Signature . . . .

Name Mr/Mrs/Ms . . . .

Address . . . .

. . . .

. . . .

. . . . Postcode . . . .

Daytime Tel No . . . .   Valid to 31/12/03

The Francis Frith Collectors' Guild
Please enrol me as a member for 12 months free of charge.

Name Mr/Mrs/Ms . . . .

Address . . . .

. . . .

. . . . Postcode . . . .

Would you like to find out more about Francis Frith?

We have recently recruited some entertaining speakers who are happy to visit local groups, clubs and societies to give an illustrated talk documenting Frith's travels and photographs. If you are a member of such a group and are interested in hosting a presentation, we would love to hear from you.

Our speakers bring with them a small selection of our local town and county books, together with sample prints. They are happy to take orders. A small proportion of the order value is donated to the group who have hosted the presentation. The talks are therefore an excellent way of fundraising for small groups and societies.

Can you help us with information about any of the Frith photographs in this book?

We are gradually compiling an historical record for each of the photographs in the Frith archive. It is always fascinating to find out the names of the people shown in the pictures, as well as insights into the shops, buildings and other features depicted.

If you recognize anyone in the photographs in this book, or if you have information not already included in the author's caption, do let us know. We would love to hear from you, and will try to publish it in future books or articles.

Our production team

Frith books are produced by a small dedicated team at offices in the converted Grade II listed 18th-century barn at Teffont near Salisbury, illustrated above. Most have worked with the Frith Collection for many years. All have in common one quality: they have a passion for the Frith Collection. The team is constantly expanding, but currently includes:

Jason Buck, John Buck, Douglas Burns, Heather Crisp, Lucy Elcock, Isobel Hall, Rob Hames, Hazel Heaton, Peter Horne, James Kinnear, Tina Leary, Hannah Marsh, Eliza Sackett, Terence Sackett, Sandra Sanger, Lewis Taylor, Shelley Tolcher, Helen Vimpany, Clive Wathen and Jenny Wathen.